Luxury Marketing Disrupted

Evolving from the 4Ps to the 4Es of Marketing

By Pamela N. Danziger

Pamela N. Danziger

Unity Marketing
206 E. Church St.
Stevens, PA 17578
717-336-1600

Copyright © 2019 Pamela N. Danziger

All rights reserved. No part of this book may be reproduced, stored in a retrieval system, or transmitted in any form by any means, electronic, mechanical, photocopying, recording or otherwise without the prior written permission of the publisher.

Table of Contents

Evolving from the 4Ps to the 4Es of Marketing 4

Marketing Disrupted 16

Marketing to HENRYs in a Brand New Style 18

    ■ CASE STUDY: De Beers 19

Experience Replaces Product 26

    ■ CASE STUDY: Apple 27

Place Becomes Everyplace 35

    ■ CASE STUDY: Chanel & Gucci 36

Price Is Now Exchange 42

    ■ CASE STUDY: Revtown 43

Promotion Is Now Evangelism 49

    ■ CASE STUDY: 1stDibs 50

Answer Marketing's Higher Calling 55

    ■ CASE STUDY: Zara & H&M 56

Pillars of New Luxury 64

Get More Insights 69

About the Author 71

Pamela N. Danziger

Luxury Marketing Disrupted

Evolving from the 4Ps to the 4Es of Marketing

The age-old, recession-immune business of luxury has been disrupted. Look no further than Paris, called the capital of luxury retail back in 2017 by the real-estate research firm Savills after it experienced the most luxury retail store openings in the world.

Then look at Paris today. It is a battleground with yellow-vested protestors in the streets. The populist protest movement started in October 2019 and continues unabated nearly a year after. In December during an epic moment in the protests, police had to fire tear gas and use water cannons to disperse the Yellow-Vest crowds on the Champs Élysées.

More recently, Hong Kong has erupted in grassroots protests against threats of political repression from mainland China. Unlike Paris, the protestors have not aimed at luxury retail, yet luxury brands potentially stand in the crosshairs. The airport had to be shut down with protests making travel unsafe. Already Hong Kong luxury watch retailers are hurting. Investment firm Savigny Partners reports Hong Kong has lost first place as the world's largest market for luxury watches to the U.S.

While other global centers of luxury have not erupted with such violent demonstrations as has Paris or Hong Kong, the luxury market is becoming a battleground nonetheless.

The primary battle lines in luxury over the coming years will be global political and market turbulence and competitors struggling for a shrinking share of consumer spending, even while the ranks of the wealthy rise. Also, luxury brands will be challenged to focus on the human dimension of the digital revolution, as they seek to find traction with the younger, digitally-powered consumers that demand it.

Market Turbulence, Slowing Sales

While publicly-traded luxury company stocks continue to perform well, the Savigny Luxury Index, which tracks the values of 18 leading luxury companies, reports that investors are losing patience. "Overall sentiment towards luxury goods has cooled, with investors putting the current round of results into the context of high valuation multiples." Savigny concludes, "Investors demand more from expensive luxury stocks," and that means more growth.

While China has been a ripe growth market for luxury brands, it is worrying everyone now, especially in light of reduced Chinese tourist spending and threats of a trade war. "China sneezes, and the world catches a cold these days," Savigny says." Retail sales in China grew at their slowest rate in 15 years in November 2018, and industrial growth was its slowest in three years. To add insult to injury, China-US trade talks are going nowhere."

French investment bank Societe General foresees similar trends, forecasting a "slowdown in the luxury sector has just started as concerns over the spending trend of affluent Chinese millennials and the impact of the Yellow Vest protest in France."

Goldman Sachs concurred and dropped its 2019 forecast for luxury industry sales growth from a previous 7 percent to 5 percent.

The investment community dislikes uncertainty, and there is plenty of it to go around. A recent survey by J.P. Morgan among ultra-high-net-worth investors (those with more than $30 million in liquid financial assets) found that 75 percent expect a recession to hit the U.S. by 2020.

Even Gucci CEO Marco Bizzarri, who sits on top of the world's fastest-growing legacy luxury brand, knows the good times can't last. "We need to recognize the fact that at a certain point we're going to slow down, we cannot keep on growing 50-60 percent per month, it's impossible," he said in a video to company employees.

And Bizzarri's prophecy was fulfilled in the second quarter 2019, when Gucci sales slowed, mainly as a result of a weaker-than-expected performance in the United States.

Rising Wealth, Growing Anxiety

What gives luxury brands hope is the growing wealth class. Those who can afford luxuries have more money than ever to spend on it.

Capgemini, in its World Wealth Report 2018, reported global high-net-worth-individual wealth rose 10.6 percent in 2017 to surpass $70 trillion, the first time it has reached this level. This follows six consecutive years of wealth gains.

Capgemini defines the HNWI as those with investible assets of $1 million or more, excluding primary residence, collectibles, consumables, and consumer durables. At its present rate, global HNWI wealth may top $100 trillion by 2025.

Credit Suisse takes a more inclusive look at the wealthy, including the value of one's primary residence and other things that Capgemini excludes. According to its calculation, the number of millionaires reached 42.2 million worldwide in 2018.

Pamela N. Danziger

The U.S. has the heaviest concentration of millionaires by far, with some 41 percent of the world's millionaires or 17.4 million of them living there. That is almost as many millionaires as live in the next largest nine countries combined. China has but 3.5 million millionaires, Japan 2.8 million, and the U.K. 2.4 million, these three being the next most prosperous countries.

But cultural tides are turning against the wealthy elite. Where wealth used to be something the affluent wore proudly, today the wealthy are retreating into their cocoons, living behind walls and going increasingly inconspicuous.

> *As the rich get richer, everybody else has fallen behind.*

Income inequality is causing resentment among the hoi polloi and anxiety to rise among the wealthy. The results can be catastrophic, as we see in France. One of the flashpoints in the Yellow-Vest protests is President Emmanuel Macron's repel of the French wealth tax imposed on households with assets valued at €1.3 million or more.

Speaking of the riots that caused shops on Paris' luxury thoroughfares to be boarded up, Mario Ortelli, managing partner of luxury advisors Ortelli & Co, told the *Business of Fashion*, "You don't want to shop at Louis Vuitton on the Champs Élysées when cars are burning on the street. You don't want to walk around with an Hermès bag when there's a violent protest happening."

The French backlash against the wealthy elite has had immediate impacts on luxury sales, which are likely to persist through 2020 with not just the wealthy Chinese but other well-heeled tourists avoiding the country. The French Finance Minister Bruno Le Maire estimated Paris has experienced a sales decline between 20 percent-40 percent as a result of the protests.

Consumers don't like uncertainty any more than investors. It isn't only fear of physical violence that will keep people from shopping in France and Hong Kong. It is psychological anxiety about what comes next.

What is happening in France and Hong Kong is but a bellwether of things to come worldwide as the wealthy grow more anxious. In response, they are becoming less conspicuous as they retreat from danger in the public square and act to secure their holdings.

The watchwords for the wealthy in 2020 will be privacy and security. This will only make it harder for luxury brands to connect with them in the future.

Adapting the Human Side of Digital Disruption

After being slow to adapt to the digital revolution, luxury brands have made extraordinary investments to play catch up. With most brands now comfortable selling their luxe online, with the notable exception of Chanel, many of the luxury players are going deeper into the digital market.

Why? Because that is where the growth is. Euromonitor International reports that luxury goods sales are growing nearly three-times faster online than in physical retail, 14 percent as compared with traditional retail at 5 percent.

Digital disrupters got an early leg up on the digital revolution, as luxury brands were slow to commit or not convinced that their customers wanted to interact digitally. This also made for strange partnerships, like that between chief competitors Richemont and Kering.

Not long after Richemont acquired digitally-native multi-brand platform Net-a-Porter and combined it with Yoox to create YNAP, which also provided e-commerce operations for seven of its chief competitor Kering's brands, Kering announced it was ending its YNAP operations partnership to develop its in-house online capability by 2020.

When that was announced, YNAP said, "This transition is a natural evolution for a large group with the scale of Kering," and pointed to the fact that Kering was already running e-commerce operations in house for Gucci, its largest brand.

But YNAP also operates online flagship stores for 26 other competing luxury brands, like Alaia, Balmain, and Ferrari. Even as YNAP remains committed to managing each online store independently and offers bespoke technology solutions for each, other big players may look to bring e-commerce operations back inside.

All the while, Richemont through YNAP continues to support sales of Kering and many other luxury brands across its multi-brand online luxury retail platforms, including Net-a-Porter, Mr Porter, Yoox, and Outnet.

Farfetch, a digital fashion marketplace that offers selections from nearly 900 fashion boutiques and brands worldwide, has similar partnerships with Burberry and Chanel, although Chanel is using Farfetch-supplied technology in its stores, not to sell online.

Last year, LVMH, parent of Louis Vuitton, launched its own multi-brand website known as 24 Sevres, now going by the name 24S.com. LVMH also maintains individual websites for its House brands.

> *Luxury brands have been slow to adapt to the human side of the digital revolution.*

But as luxury brands have all eyes on technology, they've been slower to adapt to the human side of the digital revolution. Using catchphrases like omnichannel or channel-agnostic, most organizations still run digital operations behind locked doors. That is because the technologists remain the experts on translating the brand's DNA into computer code.

SAP's Lori Mitchell-Keller explained a major hurdle for luxury brands is to maintain the perceived "cache of luxury in the online world." But the digital revolution also calls on them to enhance the human experience, as it is humans who have to interact with the brands, either digitally or physically, to make a purchase.

Programming the human dimension into luxury brands' digital and in-store systems will require managers with skill sets acquired from anthropology or sociology, not necessarily in the computer science lab or the retail management track.

Then there is the continued digital disruption coming to advertising and marketing that supports luxury brands in their mission. The winners in the future will be digital advertising platforms; the losers will be print publications.

For example, Calvin Klein announced it would pull all advertising from print media starting in February 2019 in favor of a "digital-first, socially-amplified model." While other luxury brands are not expected to make such an all-or-nothing move, luxury brands will continue to pull money out of print and shift it to digital in the future.

U.K.-based Zenith's 2019 Advertising Expenditure Forecasts reports that digital spending will be responsible for all growth in luxury advertising spending. "We forecast luxury advertising in digital media to grow by U.S. $886m between 2017 and 2019," it reports and adds that digital will account for about 33 percent of luxury's total advertising budgets.

Enter Digitally-Powered Customers

To grow, luxury brands need new customers, and today, that means millennials. The generation's sheer size -- reputed to be as large if not larger than the baby boom generation-- offers luxury brands a 20+ year supply of new customers.

Looking across this vast generational cohort, defined by Pew as 73 million strong in 2019 and born between 1981 and 1996, there is one segment in that cohort that is most important for luxury brands: the HENRYs (high-earners-not-rich-yet).

With higher incomes relative to the majority of the population, between $100k and $250k in the U.S., HENRYs hold the space above the bottom 75th percentile but below the top five percent, where luxury brand's traditional ultra-affluent customers are found. Since true affluence comes with age, the millennials aged 24-to-39 in 2020 are only now beginning to hit their stride in terms of income and wealth.

Compared with the rest of the millennial generation, the young HENRYs are better educated, more informed, and set the trends that their lower-earning peers will emulate. And even more important for the long-term prospects of legacy luxury brands, most people who reach ultra-affluent levels of income start as HENRYs in starting their careers. These are the customers that luxury brands need to identify now to nurture for future growth.

Complicating matters for luxury brands is that HENRY millennials approach the luxury market with new ideas about what luxury is, what it means to them, and how they want to participate in it. A recent Ipsos study found that 81 percent of modern luxury consumers believe the definition of luxury is rapidly changing, a fact that should be abundantly clear to luxury brands.

> *HENRYs' new ideas about luxury require luxury brands to adapt.*

HENRYs' new ideas about luxury will require fundamental shifts in what luxury brands sell and how they sell it. Some luxury brands are on it, but many other brands remain entrenched in more traditional ideas of luxury.

First and foremost, millennial HENRYs place a higher value on experiences than tangible luxury goods. "There is a fundamental shift in consumer values towards luxury experiences over things that bring happiness and well-being," reports Euromonitor, citing a survey among millennials that found over 50 percent of U.S. millennials prefer to spend money on experiences rather than things.

That means the concept of a luxury good as a status symbol is rapidly being replaced by that of a status experience or an Instagram-worthy moment. Millennial HENRYs want to start checking off the boxes on their bucket list by age 40, not wait till their 70.

Turning to their material goods' needs, millennial HENRYs are the most empowered generation ever, and thanks to technology, they have access at their fingertips to most of the products the world has to offer. They are also far more educated and informed consumers than any generation before and so can suss out the relative value of potential purchases to make decisions right for them.

Increasingly traditional luxury goods are not making the cut, as HENRYs opt for lower-priced but still premium options from brands like Everlane, Gilt, Outnet.com (the outlet site for full-priced Net-a-Porter), membership sites like RuLaLa, as well as Neiman Marcus' Last Call, Nordstrom's Rack and Saks Off 5th Avenue.

With experiences their focus, millennial HENRYs are also choosing access to luxury over ownership of it, giving rise to the gently-used luxury market and the rental model, from Rent the Runway, The RealReal, Zipcar, AirBnB and Uber. These purchases don't weigh them down with the high cost of ownership and maintenance.

Luxury brands are going to feel the conflicting push-pull from their traditional wealthy and older customers who want one type of luxury and their younger, less financially-endowed customers and potential customers who want a totally different kind of luxury. Luxury's present fortunes hang on the one, and their future depends on the other.

Luxury brands face a complicated balancing act in 2020 and beyond as they are forced to navigate potential disruption coming at them from these four macro trends. Not all will be up for the challenge.

It will require luxury brands to more effectively communicate their brands' value proposition. That takes marketing. And that too has been disrupted.

Marketing Disrupted

Marketing's disruption happened officially in 2013 when the American Marketing Association changed its definition of marketing. It went from the old 4Ps definition which most of us practicing marketers were drilled in: Product, Price, Promotion, Placement, to a new one based upon the idea of value:

> Marketing is the activity, set of institutions, and processes for creating, communicating, delivering, and exchanging offerings that have value for customers, clients, partners, and society at large.

Most marketers never got the "memo," judging from the sorry state of the retail business today. Already this year, the number of retail closings has surpassed the record set in 2018 (5,864). Through July 31, 2019, some 7,578 stores have closed, and Coresight Research predicts the total by year-end will top 12,000 closures

The retail world is changing at light speed. That calls on marketers to answer to a higher calling, one that truly reflects the changing mindset, expectations, and needs of customers. This is even more important for luxury brands whose future rests on attracting the attention and support of young HENRYs. These are the next-generation luxury customers. They are on the cutting-edge in the search for value and meaning in the consumer goods and services they purchase.

A case in point: luxury brands continue to believe that the way to market to young customers is by creating "aspiration" for the brand. The idea behind aspirational marketing is to create demand by communicating that HENRY consumers will achieve some special status or social position by acquiring the brand.

But here's news for those brands: Aspirational marketing may work for some people, but not those who actually can afford what the luxe brands are selling. HENRY consumers aren't necessarily interested in status and position. They don't need any brand to give it to them. As a result, luxury marketing must evolve from its focus on "aspiration" to one of "inspiration."

To do that, luxury marketing must inspire the HENRYs to see how the brand is meaningful and delivers a measurable value that enhances their lifestyle.

Here's how:

Marketing to HENRYs in a Brand New Style

Education and training aside, one reason we cling to the old 4Ps of marketing is its simplicity. Following that model for simplicity, Ogilvy & Mather's Brian Fetherstonhaugh has proposed a new formula, the 4Es: Experience, Everyplace, Exchange, and Evangelism. The secret is to use these 4E ideas to communicate and deliver meaningful value to the customer.

Luxury brands and the customers they serve are at the pinnacle of the consumer hierarchy. Marketing strategies and tactics based on the 4Ps make a clear statement that the brand is outmoded, old-fashioned, and worse, for the masses. To sell to the contemporary HENRY affluents, luxury marketers need to evolve to the new 4Es model of marketing where:

- Experience replaces Product
- Everyplace is the new Place
- Exchange is the new Price
- Evangelism is now Promotion

HENRY millennials are bringing changes to the luxury market that demand brands redesign their luxury marketing in this new style. Brands must reimagine, refit, and align their luxury to these new ideas and perceptions of what luxury is and where it fits into HENRYs' lifestyle now and in the future.

De Beers, the diamond industry leader, is undertaking such an effort in launching a new type of diamond – one grown in a laboratory – for a new type of customer – the self-purchasing HENRY woman.

■ CASE STUDY: De Beers

Lab-grown diamonds are now a girl's best friend

Look at any list of the most powerful advertising messages of all times and the 1948 De Beers-N.W. Ayers slogan "A Diamond Is Forever" is at the top. While many claim the tag line made the $80 billion diamond industry what it is today, advertising didn't do it alone.

The diamond's allure was further propelled in the early 50s by the seductive image of Marilyn Monroe singing an ode to the stones:

> Men grow cold as girls grow old
> And we all lose our charms in the end.
> But square-cut or pear-shaped
> These rocks don't lose their shape.
> Diamonds are a girl's best friend.

Marilyn would have been 93 years old on June 1, 2019, and she never lived long enough to experience the truth in those lyrics. But her image and that song reinforced the "A Diamond Is Forever" message back in the 50s in a deep cultural way that no paid advertising ever could have achieved.

Fast forward to today, and a hot new rock is threatening the original diamond-is-forever concept: laboratory-grown diamonds. Thanks to advances in manufacturing technology, gemstone-quality diamonds can now be industrially grown. These lab-grown diamonds are identical in composition and structure to diamonds formed naturally over the ages in the earth.

Priced lower than natural diamonds and brought to market without the collateral environmental and human damage associated with mining operations, lab-grown diamonds are increasingly the choice for the conscientious, social-justice, values-focused consumer.

And no consumer is more conscientious or values-focused than 19-39-year-old HENRY millennials, who are the primary target for the diamond industry's flagship product: engagement rings.

Diamonds disrupted
As of yet, the lab-grown diamond industry is tiny compared to mined diamonds, representing less than 1 percent of the global market for rough diamonds,

according to estimates by Morgan Stanley. But that is about to change.

"The introduction of hot-forged jewelry-grade diamonds, identical to those the earth takes eons to mete out, has sweeping implications for the $80 billion industry that has relied on the perceived scarcity of mined diamonds to drive up value," said Amish Shah, president of R. A. Riam Group, which offers mined-diamond jewelry and ALTR Created Diamonds selling the lab-grown variety.

"Sales of lab-created diamonds, now estimated at $150 million, are expected to increase to $1 billion by 2020 and outpace growth in mined diamonds, which have been in decline," Shah says.

Until now, the mined-diamond industry – and De Beers – have been pushing back against the disruptive lab-grown producers with the claim that only mined diamonds are the real thing. Lab-grown are fake pretenders. But that argument doesn't hold water.

"Lab-created diamonds and earth-mined diamonds are exactly the same thing. It's like ice on a frozen lake and ice created in your freezer. One is created by a natural process and one by a man-made process. But in the end, they are identical in all ways down to the atomic level," said Gary LaCourt, CEO of Forever Companies that markets alternative and lab-grown diamond brands Diamond Nexus, 1215 Diamond, and Forever Artisans.

Pamela N. Danziger

De Beers sees the writing on the wall

No company stands more to lose than De Beers, which controls 35-40 percent of the mined-diamond market. After years of disavowing the authenticity of lab-grown diamonds, De Beers has done a 180° about-face and just announced it is launching a line of man-made diamonds under the Lightbox Jewelry brand.

"Lightbox will transform the lab-grown diamond sector by offering consumers a lab-grown product they have told us they want but aren't getting: affordable fashion jewelry that may not be forever but is perfect for right now," Bruce Cleaver, CEO of De Beers Group said in a statement. "Our extensive research tells us this is how consumers regard lab-grown diamonds – as a fun, pretty product that shouldn't cost that much – so we see an opportunity that's been missed by lab-grown diamond producers."

Adding to the fun element in the Lightbox Jewelry line will be an emphasis on colored pink and blue stones to complement the traditional clear white diamonds. Prices will start at $200 for a quarter-carat stone to $800 for one-carat. These prices, however, don't include the cost of the jewelry setting, which will initially include earrings and necklace designs, but not rings.

The company release does not specifically mention the primary target for the Lightbox Jewelry line. But it is clearly meant for self-purchasing women, not men buying diamonds for women. Strategically, Lightbox won't threaten De Beers' core engagement ring market, since initially it is not even offering rings in the collection. To that end, De Beers distinguishes its mined-diamond offering as "forever," as in "A Diamond Is Forever," compared to its Lightbox style-savvy alternative as "for right now."

It also is a smart move that DeBeers calls Lightbox "fashion jewelry," positioning it as the more affordable alternative to natural, mined-diamond "fine jewelry" quality. The official industry distinction between fine and fashion jewelry is that fashion doesn't have precious gemstones or precious metals (other than plating), while fine jewelry is made with natural precious gemstones and metals.

As De Beers moves Lightbox Jewelry into the market, it guides its customers: "If you want fashion jewelry, Lightbox is your choice. If you want precious fine jewelry, then Forevermark and De Beers Jewellers is for you."

Millennial HENRYs want different options

De Beers may not be able to sell that distinction, however, as millennials have already shown that they aren't buying into the idea that a lab-grown diamond is in any way inferior to its mined counterpart. Quite the contrary.

Among consumers in general, and millennials specifically, mined-diamonds have a bad reputation for the high human cost and environmental damage that mining operations entail. This generation is fixated on responsible sourcing and manufacturing of the products they buy. Lab-grown diamonds meet that demand, while mined-diamonds fall short.

"Millennials want to know that the products they buy aren't harming anybody in their production. This is across all consumer products," said Marty Hurwitz, CEO of MVI Marketing, whose company recently conducted a study among 1,000+ American consumers, aged 21-40 years, across all income ranges with half having household incomes of $50,000 or higher.

"That's why companies are tracing chain of custody and providing transparency of supply chain. There isn't a product in Whole Foods, Nordstrom or Walmart, for that matter, that isn't being traced in case someone asks. Millennials are driving this trend," Hurwitz says.

In that survey, nearly 70 percent of consumers said "Yes," they would consider a lab-grown diamond for the center stone in an engagement ring if they were shopping or shopping with someone for an engagement ring. That represents an increase of 13 percentage points in only one year. "Millennials are telling the jewelry industry this is a product they are interested in and will come into the store to look at it," Hurwitz adds.

De Beers moves to control the diamond narrative
By embracing lab-grown diamonds and calling it their own, De Beers is disrupting the industry's stance against the

numerous startups eating away at their market dominance. These brands include Ada Diamonds, ALTR Created Diamonds, Diamond Foundry, New Dawn Diamonds and Pure Grown among others, though no market-share leader has emerged as yet.

Rather than fight the rising tide against laboratory-grown diamonds which has found a consumer market-ready, willing and able to embrace it, De Beers is getting in early to take a leadership position in an emerging category with no clear-cut leader. Now it will have one, with De Beers' mighty marketing muscle moving in to define the category and establish its positioning against the lab-grown upstarts, as well as elevating its mined-diamond precious jewelry offering.

De Beers helped make diamonds what they are today. Next, De Beers is going to try to make laboratory-diamonds what they will be tomorrow: a fun fashion pretender to the real, rare, precious, natural, "forever" diamond.

And as it did with diamonds throughout its 130-year history, De Beers is aiming to become the market leader by using its power to establish prices for both the mined and laboratory-diamond markets.

Its Lightbox Jewelry prices are way below current levels in the industry today and given advances in technology and production processes, the costs to produce man-made stones will only continue to fall. By establishing a low-price alternative to the real thing, De Beers will aim to drive up the prices for its natural stones. It's a very smart and bold move and one that few saw coming.

Experience Replaces Product

We all talk about the experiential economy, and it's easy to market a brand when it's an experience, like dining, travel, or spas. But what about all the luxury goods brands? How do they turn their products into an experience for the customer? Yes, customer service is important, but it takes more than that.

> *Retail becomes the place for people to share experiences with brands and products.*

To turn luxury goods products into experiences for the customer, companies need to do a deep dive into understanding the feelings that drive customers to make a purchase, and no 'big data' or quantitative data can provide that answer. It requires getting up close and personal with the customers to understand the special experiences they get from the brand and its products.

Brands that understand this new experiential dimension in the marketing formula include Stitch Fix and Trunk Club, both of which put a personal stylist to work to select complete outfits according to the woman's or man's style profile and deliver care packages to try on in the privacy and comfort of one's home.

Or Laudi Vidni which involves the customer in the creation of their handbag, specifying the style, leather, lining, and do-dads to create their own personal design.

Or Project Gravitas which started with a simple idea, giving women the perfect LBD (little black dress) designed to enhance her body shape, with the added confidence of a shapewear lining so that she always looks her best.

All these brands turn the chore of shopping and buying into a personal experience for the customer.

■ CASE STUDY: Apple

How Apple has evolved in the experience economy

For the latest and greatest in personal technology, everybody looks to Apple. They lead the pack in creating innovative, user-friendly computing products. And the company takes the same innovative, forward-looking approach to retail.

Yet people think of Apple as a product-first technology company, when in fact it is a hybrid that seamlessly combines products and services into a new kind of company that is ideally suited to the evolving experience economy.

It transforms its products into experiences and delivers those product experiences through a new kind of retailing model that elevates the Apple Store from a place to buy things into a destination to have meaningful, important experiences.

As innovative as Apple is as a product company, so too, it is innovative as a retailer. That's why retailers across the board need to listen and learn from Apple. But my experience is that unless you're a retailer that competes in Apple's vertical, like Verizon and Best Buy, what Apple is doing at retail is not really on your radar unless it is as a customer.

With so many struggling retailers trying to respond effectively to the emerging experience economy, retailers in every vertical can learn from Apple. Here are three important lessons about its experience-based retail business model that Apple has implemented and retailers across the board from grocery, fashion, home, and the rest need to understand too:

- **Become a place to learn**

In the experience economy, consumers take very seriously and enjoy their experiences leading up to a purchase. In research with consumers, I am amazed how much time, effort, and consideration the time-starved, multi-tasking HENRYs devote to pre-purchase research for purchases both large and small. They are relentless in gathering all the information they can about buying the things that matter to them, and luxury goods matter more than most other things.

The secret is not pushing more marketing messages out, but using marketing to draw HENRYs in. Marketers have an awesome opportunity to provide the information their customers crave. That requires luxury brands not push out information as a marketing ploy, but to use the information to draw them in. It's got to arouse curiosity and be meaningful, useful information that will give them an edge, not marketing fluff which they can smell a mile away.

"Today at Apple" is its answer to providing meaningful, useful information tailored to the interests and needs of its customers. Sure, a lot of the "Today at Apple" educational programming is aimed at helping its customers learn how to use its technology. But much more importantly, it also exposes them to new experiences in music, art, design, and photography, broadening their perspectives, and delivering information from subject-matter experts who educate and inform them, not shill Apple products.

Recently I've been working in home furnishings retail and have learned that decorating a livable, comfortable, and stylish room is not as easy as portrayed on 30-second Wayfair commercials or hour-long HGTV shows. Retail home furnishings customers are eager to learn more about home design. A furniture or home furnishings retailer should be a place where consumers get that information so that they can become better designers of their home space and better home furnishings consumers.

But the same thinking can apply to any other category of retail, from fashion, grocery, gifts, books, jewelry, beauty, crafts, office supplies, pharmacy. HENRYs today – the customers' luxury retailers hope to serve – are information sponges. Retailers should think beyond providing information just about their merchandise to providing information about the customers' lifestyles and their dreams that the merchandise they sell makes possible.

Meet that higher-level need with meaningful information, above and beyond the lower-level drive to sell more products, and you will bind that customer for life. In the experiential economy, retailers need a similar "Today at Apple" strategy to serve their customers' lifestyle interests, not just their product-specific needs.

- **Become a place to gather**

Now with nearly 500 stores worldwide and after 15 years of retail behind it, Apple is re-envisioning its stores as "Town Squares," places where people can come together, learn and experience, as well as places to buy product.

The redesign is more than just window dressing, though it includes that, like adding living trees to the modernistic store design and changing the name of its Genius Bars to "Genius Groves." It transcends the idea of the four walls of the physical store from a place to display products in anticipation of a sale into an environment where people will gather.

The Apple store becomes a place for people to share experiences in a community of collaboration. "The store becomes one with the community," Angela Ahrendts, Apple's then senior vice president of retail, explained in an interview with The Verge. "The over-arching vision of the future of Apple retail … is what do we want Apple's role in the community to be?" That goal, according to Ahrendts, is to make Apple stores forums for collaboration.

This is a powerful idea: the store as a place for people to share experiences in a community of collaboration.

"As we need less or want less, stores that figure out how to make you go there – where buying is secondary to the experience, but not the focus of the experience – are going to be important places," Ken Nisch, chairman of retail design firm JGA shares, as he points to both Starbucks and Apple as retailers that do just that.

"It used to be that lifestyle retail was the ultimate. Now it is concept retail, shops like American Girl Place and Selfridges," Nisch shared. "These are stores at the top of the retail pyramid that have built a community. They become part of the community."

Malls, as they try to figure out how to bring customers back again, are beginning to understand the need to become vital members of their communities, not just places for people to buy stuff. Malls need to become community centers where people come together to share and connect, like Main Street USA, and the retailers and other local businesses which make their home there. People are looking for places where community experiences can occur.

- **Become a place to serve**

As retailers evolve in this digital age, one aspect of retail never goes out of style: good old-fashioned customer service. Apple is on the cutting edge of the digital transformation in retail, but it remains committed to delivering a personal experience in its stores.

Modeling its customer service approach after luxury hotelier Ritz-Carlton's Steps of Service guidelines, Apple adapted its own steps of service, creating an acronym that appropriately spells A-P-P-L-E:

> **(A)** Approach customers with a personalized warm welcome – "May I help you" is not helpful at all for retail. Retail personnel need a new script that really connects with people and gets them to answer beyond, "No, just looking."
>
> **(P)** Probe politely to understand customers' needs – The Apple sales philosophy is not to sell, but

rather to help customers solve problems. Its stated goal is to "delight the customers." Forbes.com contributor Steve Denning explained, "Apple has grasped that making money is the result of the firm's actions, not the goal. By delighting the customer, Apple ends up making more money than it would if it set out to make money."

(P) Present a solution for the customer to take home today – That solution may be a new piece of Apple gear or a problem solved by one of the Apple Geniuses or pictures taken on a guided Photo Walk.

(L) Listen for and resolve any issues or concerns – And when all else fails, Apple has developed a guide for its sales associates called "Emergency First Aid for Emotional Customers" that is heavy on feeling and empathy, such as "Listen and limit responses to simple reassurances," and "Acknowledge the customer's underlying reaction."

(E) End with a fond farewell and an invitation to return – As important as customers' first impression is, so also is the feeling that they have when they leave the store. So Apple trains on both the hellos and goodbyes to have customers take away good feelings, good memories and look forward to their return.

Christopher Ramey, of retail advisory firm Retail Rescue, says, "Most luxury hotels train their employees every day, but my experience with retailers is they train every year, if that often," Ramey said. "The disconnect is obvious."

Ramey further notes the importance of providing sales associates with scripts for customer interactions at the opening, closing and throughout the service process, just as Apple has done. "Communications are powerful, and today there can be little latitude for the salesperson to be flexible with words."

While people tend to think of Apple as a product company, it thinks differently about itself. "We think of Apple Retail as Apple's largest product," Ahrendts said.

Apple retail stores generate more sales per square foot ($5,546), according to eMarketer, than any other U.S. retailer. That's nearly twice as much as Tiffany & Company ($2,951) and way ahead of Lululemon, Michael Kors, Kate Spade and RH/Restoration Hardware which are among the top 10 retailers based on sales per square foot. For Apple, the store experiences impact not only on sales and branding, but in personal customer connection make the difference.

Retailers that have yet to figure out the new retail business model for the experience economy, and most still haven't, need to look to Apple for inspiration. Instead of "apple for teacher," it is Apple IS teacher.

Place Becomes Everyplace

The concept of Everyplace includes the idea of allowing customers to engage with brands on their own terms, through their own paths to purchase, whether it be online, in-store, at home or by phone.

> *Take the customer experience directly to the consumer, face-to-face, person-to-person.*

Many luxury brands have given into this idea of Everyplace by selling their goods online, but they've tended to do it kicking and screaming, rather than embracing the opportunity to make their Everyplace meaningful and memorable.

And it doesn't have to be only via the Internet, with its many different platforms (mobile, tablet, computer) to support. It can be taking the customer experience directly to the customer, face-to-face, person-to-person.

For example, custom-menswear brand J. Hilburn employs over 3,000 stylists across the country to meet with the customer to do personal fittings and give fashion advice in order to help select the right style and fabrication to suit the man and his lifestyle.

Or Lincoln Motor Cars, which offers its clients a pickup-and-delivery service whenever their cars need repairs. And this is offered across all its brands and through every

Lincoln dealer. It is all part of "The Lincoln Way" of delivering services and experiences to its customers; in other words, Lincoln has evolved into the 4Es way of marketing.

■ CASE STUDY: Chanel & Gucci
Luxury Brands Evolving Through Tech-Powered Personalized Experiences

Gucci and Chanel are using the power of customers' smartphones to deliver more personalized and human-enhanced service to their customers.

Gucci has launched a Florence-based call center, with five more to follow by 2020. The call center provides the expertise of Gucci's finest shop assistants to customers throughout the world anywhere and anytime.

And Chanel's new Soho beauty showroom, called Atelier Beauté Chanel, is crafting new ways to enhance customers' in-store shopping experience with technology. And my bet is what Chanel learns in this beauty concept store will translate into future tech-powered shopping experiences in its fashion boutiques as well.

Both companies are trying to unlock the value of the physical store by delivering expert personalized service to the customer in a way that customers feel most comfortable—with their smartphones in hand.

Customers still crave the shop experience

This is an opportunity that Sarah Willersdorf, Boston Consulting Group's partner and managing director, identified in the company's most recent study, entitled "True-Luxury Global Consumer Insight," conducted with Altagamma.

"The store is critical across all age groups," she shared with me. "But it needs to be combined with digital. Those brands that have stores and sales associates have an asset that any company that's purely online doesn't have."

In that survey, mono-brand stores are the preferred place for true-luxury consumers worldwide to shop. True-luxury consumers are defined as those who have spent a threshold amount in specific categories of luxury, with an average total annual spend of €39,000 (~$44,000).

Nearly one-third of these customers (30%) made a luxury purchase most recently in a mono-brand store, with online (21%) and high-end department stores (19%) following.

Consumers are drawn to stores first by the ability to touch and try on product, the luxury environment, and the product range available there. But personal service by sales associates is growing in importance, according to the latest survey.

The challenge, as Willersdorf sees it, is for luxury mono-brand stores to remain relevant in an increasingly online environment. Gucci and Chanel's latest efforts are showing how.

Putting Gucci expertise into the customers' hand

Starting with a 25,000-square-foot call center outside of Florence staffed by 150 highly-trained service professionals, Gucci is trying to give shoppers "a direct connection to the Gucci community that is seamless, always accessible, personalized experience," Marco Bizzarri, Gucci's chairman and chief executive officer, told the *Financial Times*. Plans are to expand the call centers worldwide to include 500 assistants in New York, Tokyo, Seoul, Shanghai and Singapore by 2020.

Shoppers can interact with call-center assistants by phone, email or live chat and those assistants are encouraged to develop personal relationships with shoppers, just like a personal store assistant would.

Gucci is placing a lot of emphasis on the call-center initiative, called Gucci 9, to drive more traffic to stores and more engagement with the brand that will ultimately grow sales. It puts Gucci everyplace the customer is.

Bizzarri said that through the call centers the company will "explore the best ways to optimize the remote client experience," which is critical in the rapidly shifting preferences customers have for interacting with luxury brands.

The new mobile-enabled access gives in-store customers more personalized service options if in-store staff are unavailable or they desire information or products beyond what the store carries. In addition, luxury shoppers are increasingly going to the store to touch and feel, then completing their purchases online afterwards. This new service facilitates that behavior.

"Consumers want to go into luxury retail spaces for easy-access consultation and experience, then quickly and seamlessly make purchases, create wish lists, schedule delivers and get follow-up information," shares Christine Andrukonis, founder and senior partner of Notion Consulting, a firm that advises companies on transformational change.

Chanel's Atelier Beauté blends in-person service with digital experiences

Opened this past January in Soho and the first of its kind, the Atelier Beauté Chanel concept store is noteworthy as a place that shifts the focus in retail from selling products to creating an immersive branded experience. It invites shoppers into the world of beauty that is Chanel.

What wowed Andrukonis and her team in a recent visit to the store was how seamlessly mobile shopping was integrated into the personal shopping experience.

"When we arrived, the Chanel team told us to put all of our belongings into lockers, but to keep our mobile phones with us. They said that was the only tool we would need," she shares. Then the assistants helped set up their accounts on the Chanel web-enabled app to get product information, application tips and to save favorite products for shopping later.

She further explained that the store assistants put no pressure on them to buy products but used the time spent to make them feel comfortable and to build a relationship of trust with the brand.

"It was clear the Chanel team was taking the long view and building relationships that could become valuable assets in the future," adds Kate DiChristopher-Yuen, a member of Notion's team.

The Atelier Beauté is an experiment for Chanel to reinvent the way customers engage with the brand, and it goes beyond just driving sales.

"Yes, it can be a way to increase sales and engagement," Andrukonis believes, but more than that, it is a pilot to gauge customer interest, gain insights to further build brand loyalty and unlock the potential in new consumer segments.

"It goes above and beyond the actual retail location with learnings that are more conceptual in order for the brand to navigate a new course or business model," she believes.

That is what Andrukonis sees here. "This type of retail experimentation and reinvention is spanning all channels for luxury brands from free-standing locations to department stores."

New customer expectations drive new rules of engagement

Gucci and Chanel are both stepping beyond the constraints of physical retail through technology to be everyplace the customer is. But at the same time the technology is unlocking the power of person-to-person physical retail.

"Today's luxury consumer wants the personalization of the human interaction mixed with the efficiency and speed of technology," Andrukonis says.

These bold experiments, combining the human element with technology's power, will lead these brands to new learnings that will inevitably result in more innovations to come.

"For brands to deliver this kind of experience, it sometimes requires an about-face across every element of their business from its vision/mission, leadership, structure, talent and capabilities and everything in between," Andrukonis believes.

Speaking to what Gucci and Chanel are doing, Andrukonis says, "Achieving this kind of modern shopping experience requires companies to be strategic, agile and ready to test, learn and grow at record-breaking speeds."

Price Is Now Exchange

Retail thought-leader Robin Lewis has bemoaned the race to the bottom caused by retailers' reliance on price as the driver for engagement. Without doubt, price still matters, even among the affluent with discretion to spend. But for the highest potential customers, the absolute price takes a back seat to value, as they are perfectly willing, and able, to pay when real value is there.

> *Exchange is the entire value experience a customer derives through the process of engaging with the brand.*

Exchange involves more than just money; it is the entire value experience a customer derives through the process of engaging with the brand. Part of the exchange can be respect for the customer's time, which is at a real premium among the affluent. It can be special insider knowledge or know-how that helps customers navigate their lives. MAC cosmetics expertly delivers expertise through makeup lessons and professional application.

Or it can be a pay-it-forward gift of something meaningful that is passed along, as Toms gives a pair of shoes to children in need for every pair of shoes bought, Warby Parker's 'buy-a-pair/give-a-pair' eyeglass offer or FEED bags which gives meals to the hungry in exchange for each bag sold.

Or it can be as simple as a meaningful thank you that makes the customer feel appreciated. Beekman 1802, the goats milk soap company founded by the Beekman Boys Brent Ridge and Josh Kilmer-Purcell, greets its Facebook followers every morning with a beautiful picture, often several of the Beekman farm. It's a personal way of saying thank you to their "neighbors," what the company calls its customers. Further engagement becomes a no-brainer.

■ CASE STUDY: Revtown

Revtown offers luxury denim at affordable prices
Into an already crowded jean market, how can Revtown breakthrough? That was my question to founder and CEO Henry Stafford when I learned about his Pittsburgh-based startup Revtown. His answer was simple, "We all wear jeans, and everybody buys jeans. All of us in this company have been wearing jeans every single day to work for years, but we didn't love the product. If we could make jeans people actually loved, then people would buy our jeans."

Stafford says he grew up in the jean business, having originally launched his career in denim at American Eagle Outfitters, then moving on to Under Armour for six years. In founding Revtown, he is joined by other Under Armour alums, including Steve Battista, former senior vice president of creative with the company, and Matt Maasdam, the former head of the company's e-commerce unit.

Together the team defined the challenge, "How do we take the experience that we had building athletic apparel and put that same mentality into designing an amazing pair of jeans?"

The need: Jeans people want to wear at home

In researching the market, they found people aged 20-to-40 years were wearing jeans 5 out of 7 days a week, but the problem was as soon as they got home, they were taking their jeans off and pulling on something more comfortable. Men were changing into training pants or athletic shorts and women into yoga pants.

"We set a challenge to our design team to make high quality, premium-designed jeans that had to be comfortable and mobile enough to rival anything in the athletic world. That took over a year," Stafford says.

The key to the design process, they discovered, was the jean's fabrication and they had to go a mill outside Milan, Italy to find it. "It all comes down to the fabric and material development. We came up with Decade Denim fabric on which to build our jeans," Stafford explains.

"Our fabric offers great mobility, great comfort, and it's also woven with the strongest fibers that are used in apparel today, so it is incredibly durable. The fabrication is our innovation. There is nothing like it out there in the denim industry," he continues.

The opportunity: Premium look at an affordable price

With the right fabric in hand, for which Stafford adds they pay a premium price, they turned to a factory in Guatemala. "Our jeans are cut, sewn, and washed by our manufacturing partner who's made over 150 million pairs of jeans. They make great products there, and they do incredible washes. They are enabling us to scale quickly which is critical to our lean-operating, speed-to-market model," Stafford says, adding that manufacturing in this hemisphere was critical in the decision.

The efficiencies achieved through its business model allows Revtown to price its premium jeans at a flat $79 per pair, which means they can compete with mass-brands like Levi's and Gap on one end and premium brands found in department stores and specialty boutiques on the other.

In the jean market today, Stafford sees the opportunity for Revtown to use a fast-fashion approach but to deliver high-quality products with it. "There is too much product out there where people are getting gouged because the model is so inefficient that the prices are way too high. We wanted to break through, so the team shares that passion to create something innovative and efficient," he says.

Revtown's business model, which Stafford says is another important innovation in the denim industry, makes that $79 price point possible. "Most every denim company out there does about 90 percent of their revenue on 10 percent of the SKUs. The remainder of the SKUs are inefficiency," he explains.

"For us, it's very simple; we just focus on the top 10 percent. We offer the best colors, the best washes. We don't have inventory sitting in dead stores or warehouses. When we have demand, we cut, sew, wash the product and that ultimately allows us to keep inventories lean, react to consumer demand and to be in size and stock very quickly," he continues.

Taking Revtown jeans to market

Under Revtown's lean-and-mean business model, which comes naturally to co-founder Maasdam, who served 14 years as a Navy SEAL, the company will launch with a men's jean line in two basic styles, Sharp for a more refined look and Automatic for "any guy, any time, any place," the company describes. Filling out the men's line will be a selection of four casual Pima cotton shirt styles. A women's product line with the same DNA will be offered later this year.

The bedroom is the new dressing room.

Revtown launched direct-to-consumer via e-commerce in keeping with its speed-to-market model. "It's no secret that e-commerce is growing far greater than any other channel of distribution out there and it will continue to grow," Stafford says.

"We look at consumer products and consumer experiences as two different things. I believe people will leave their homes to go to an experience. But they want products delivered to them at home. They want to touch and feel that product for the first time at home and reduce the friction of having to get into the car and go to the mall. The bedroom is the new dressing room," he says.

Revtown also has an answer to the subscription model that is becoming so ubiquitous in fashion e-commerce today, called the Crate. Rather than signing up for a regular shipment of new products, the customer can order a new wardrobe, once and done.

"We will give you the convenience to update your wardrobe immediately. Pick four things, and we will throw in the fifth shirt on us, and in three clicks you have a new wardrobe: a couple of pairs of jeans and three shirts. We think it's a great way for people to update their wardrobe quickly and refresh things. And it is also incredible gift-giving," Stafford explains and adds that at $228 the price of a Crate is less than one would pay for a pair of designer jeans at a department store.

"We think that's an amazing ridiculous price for the consumer and we are happy to provide that. In our lean-operating model, it enables us to be efficient so we can put all that money back into the consumer's pocket," he shares.

Revtown's story

In concluding our discussion, Stafford explains that being based in Pittsburgh, a Rust Belt town that is experiencing a renaissance through new industries, is an important part of the company's story. "Among this group, we all grew up in Rust Belt towns. It's part of the fabric of America. And we see denim as the iconic American fabric," he says.

So in naming the company – Revtown – three words kept coming up in their plans for the business:

- Revitalizing the jean market with a new business model,
- Revolutionizing the way someone buys jeans, and
- Reveling, or celebrating why they are in business.

"'Town' is because we are really proud of the towns that we're from and what that means," Stafford continues.

"Pittsburg is a hard-working town. It's an innovative town. So that's where we came up with the name 'Revtown,'" he concludes, adding, "This is a fun business. We get to make product and market it and sell it. And that's fun, and we revel in the fact that we can do that."

Promotion Is Now Evangelism

By making the brand experience meaningful and the exchange valuable, brands can tap the potential of its customers to evangelize the brand.

> *Brands must tap the potential of its customers to evangelize the brand.*

While luxury brands are wedded to the idea of traditional paid advertising and celebrity endorsements, creating individual brand evangelists that will spread the word about the brand is the highest mark of engagement. This form of evangelism is the ultimate in the new expression of marketing promotion. It's activated through content marketing, social media, traditional public relations, influencer blog posts, and through good, old-fashioned word-of-mouth marketing.

That WOM is profoundly effective goes without question. In survey after survey of B2C and B2B companies, word-of-mouth is ranked among the most important marketing strategies. The Word of Mouth Marketing Association puts numbers on its impact: WOM drives 13 percent of sales, two-thirds of which is offline talking and sharing and only one-third social media-driven. But for success, it takes planning and organizational commitment, not leaving it up to chance.

Apple is one of the most effective brands in turning its customers into Evangelists. Outdoor-brand Patagonia cemented its engagement with its brand loyalists in its "Don't Buy This Jacket" advertisement that encouraged its customers to think responsibly before buying new products. It underscored the brand's core value of quality and lifelong performance. It was such a remarkable program, it got a lot of people talking.

Beekman 1802's daily exchange of life on the farm pictures invites their neighbors into Josh and Brent's lives. It is a great example of brand evangelism designed to pull people in, rather than promotions that push out strong-armed marketing messages. Because the pictures are so remarkably beautiful, Beekman neighbors want to pass these inspiring photos along to their neighbors. Brent and Josh reject the 'lifestyle brand' label, in favor of being a "living brand." And so the story of the Beekman 1802 brand is spread.

▪ CASE STUDY: 1stDibs

1stdibs is designers' best friend, now it wants to be consumers'

1stdibs is an international online purveyor of antiques and one-of-a-kind furniture, decorative accessories and collectible objets d'art. Originally launched to serve the needs of designers for unique, collectible items for the lifestyles of the rich and famous, now it is looking more broadly to the satisfying the collecting passion of a broader consumer market – the HENRYs.

"The race for the $50 online business is already won by Amazon. But the race for $5,000 is still on. 1stdibs wants to win that one," says David Rosenblatt, CEO of 1stdibs. They are well on their way with an average order size of $3,000 – a price point that many HENRYs can trade up to when tempted to satisfy their collecting passion.

If you are unfamiliar with 1stdibs, don't blame yourself. Rosenblatt didn't know the company either when he was first approached by private-equity group Benchmark to take the reins after it made a sizeable investment in the company.

"The first person I called was my own interior designer who I was in the middle of a project with and asked him about it. He said, 'Half your apartment is from this company.' So I was immediately interested," he told me.

1stdibs then

1stdibs started life in 2001 and overnight became interior designers' best friend. Founder Michael Bruno got his inspiration browsing the Paris Flea Market, the world's largest, where the finest European antiques and 20th-century design are found. He saw the opportunity to bring those resources to the rest of the world through an online marketplace.

So Bruno partnered with some Paris dealers and built a website to list their products. Interior designers immediately came on board, as they realized they didn't have to travel to Paris to shop for their customers. More dealers in the U.S. and throughout Europe followed, and a thriving under-the-radar business was born serving interior designers and cognoscenti seeking distinctive one-of-a-kind objects to decorate their homes.

Rosenblatt joined 1stdibs in 2012 after selling the online advertising company DoubleClick to Google where he served as president of display advertising for a year. With his internet advertising credentials, he was a prime candidate for 1stdibs, which at the time was largely an advertising platform for its dealer/partners who paid a monthly fee in exchange for the right to list items. "We were like Craigslist," he says.

That changed as Rosenblatt led the move from an advertising medium to a full e-commerce marketplace. "Our mission is to create a global marketplace for the best design in the world," he explains. "Today that means e-commerce. It's the way people want to buy. It works across all time zones and allows us to create lots of advantages for our buyers and sellers that don't exist in an advertising model."

1stdibs now

One of the values that 1stdibs gives its buyers and sellers is an assurance of authenticity and provenance in the things it sells, unlike eBay. "Only authorized dealers can list items, no individuals. And in order to list, a dealer or brand needs to pass a comprehensive application in the vetting process. We are highly curated on the supply side," he describes.

In order to stay on 1stdibs, dealers must also maintain a high service record, as they handle fulfillment of orders and pay 1stdibs a commission on sales. He adds that the company has more sellers from outside the U.S., primarily Europe, than they do inside the U.S.

Today 1stdibs has over 500,000 products listed from several thousand dealers worldwide who serve buyers in 50-plus countries. Originally servicing primarily the interior design trade, 1stdibs claims 40,000 registered designers among its loyal followers. But where designers lead, in-the-know consumers follow.

Today designers represent only about 40 percent of its business, with consumers making up the lion's share. "We have about five million visits to the site each month," Rosenblatt shares.

What draws these collecting-inspired consumers to 1stdibs is easy to understand. "We are a marketplace of one-of-a-kind luxury objects," he says, noting that besides furniture and decorative objects for the home, 1stdibs also offers art, jewelry, vintage fashion and now contemporary artisan design.

"Most people want authenticity in their lives, and most especially in their homes. Home is the expression of one's personality and interests. The objects in our marketplace are different than what everyone else has. Our customers don't want their homes to look like a page out of a catalog or be the same furnishings you can buy in a furniture store. All five million of our customers can buy something truly unique and different on 1stdibs," Rosenblatt continues.

To keep its edge, which Rosenblatt describes as a "competition of aesthetics," 1stdbibs has branched out to the artisans and craft makers into contemporary design. "We see the opportunity to help these artisans come to market in the same way we saw the need for dealers selling antiques and 20th-century objects ten years ago. There is an explosion of interest in contemporary design among interior designers and consumers today."

As he grows the company, Rosenblatt takes a broader view of the role 1stdibs plays in the luxury goods market. "One way we view 1stdibs is as a marketplace for luxury design," he says. "But we are on the cutting edge of the migration of luxury into the digital realm."

With a history that started with antiques, then into 20th-century design, and now contemporary design, art, jewelry, and vintage fashion, 1stdibs spans a range of luxury consumers' interests. "We are a vehicle for the migration of the luxury market as a whole from offline to online."

In first joining 1stdibs, Rosenblatt was struck by the power and potential of its business model to satisfy the cravings of luxury-inspired consumers for unique objects that reflected their personal passion. "I saw the discrepancy between how important 1stdibs was to designers and the low profile it had in the consumer market in general. We are planning to change that," he says.

Answer Marketing's Higher Calling

The time is now to answer to marketing's higher calling by evolving from the 4Ps to the 4Es approach. It takes more than just a shift in tactics; it requires a complete reset of how you look at your customers and the ways you engage with them.

Essential to the process is to talk with customers in a personal way and engage them in discussions about how they view the brand and ways they want to participate with them. This is the raw 'material' from which real insights can lead to innovation.

Help for Marketers

Today's affluent HENRY customer is looking for a more understated expression of style, not the arm candy that ultra-expensive bags represent. They crave luxury in a brand new style. Rather than conspicuous consumption and status symbols that proclaim one's wealth, the HENRYs are embracing brands that give them bragging rights to how smart and conscientious a shopper he or she is.

For example, affluent New York City HENRYs recently adopted the $70 Uniqlo Ultra-Lite Down Jacket as their 'It' coat, rather than one from a tony Madison Avenue furrier. This jacket is cool and chic in an anti-status, conscientious-consumption, smart-shopper way. Plus it keeps them toasty warm on windy New York City streets.

■ CASE STUDY: Zara & H&M
In Fast Fashion, Zara wins with the 4Es and H&M loses with the 4Ps

Fast fashion is the darling of the fashion retail today. Whereas women's clothing store sales have declined 2.6 percent from 2016-2018 in the U.S., a recent report from Hitwise shows the fast fashion market has grown 21 percent worldwide over the past three years.

Two brands are the leaders in the fast-fashion market: H&M and Zara, an Inditex brand. Given that both are international brands, it's hard to draw line-by-line comparisons for the U.S./Americas' market. But here is what you need to know: Zara/Inditex is growing – 15.5 percent in 2018 on top of 15.6 percent in 2017 – whereas H&M sales declined 6.1 percent from 2017 to 2018. H&M operates 578 stores in the U.S., while Zara operates about 350 stores here, plus 66 Zara Home stores.

FIT Assistant Profession of Technology Shelley E. Kohan and I shared our perspectives on the two brands and why Zara is doing so much better than H&M while operating in the same basic segment.

> *H&M hasn't evolved from the 4Ps, while Zara has adopted the 4Es model of marketing.*

Our conclusion: H&M hasn't evolved beyond the 4Ps model of marketing – Product, Price, Promotion & Placement – while Zara is operating under the 4Es model in line with the expectations, wants and needs of today's customers.

For Zara, Experiences have replaced Product; Exchange is its Price; Evangelism is how it Promotes and Everyplace is where it's at.

H&M still thinks product is king; Zara knows it's experience

In the new retail economy, experience matters more than product in the mind of the shopper. H&M has an overabundance of product to worry about, including a reported stockpile of $4.3 billion of unexciting, uninspired, unsold inventory. All that unsold product clogging up the stores needs tending. They are a mess.

Zara, by contrast, understands that customers want to experience shopping, not just buy products. Zara is an excellent purveyor of product, but it also capitalizes on the store experience by continuously offering reasons for customers to visit the stores and catch the hottest trends at affordable prices. Zara has created a loyal customer whose visit frequency is about six times per year, as compared to other retailers in the contemporary fashion market of two-three times per year.

The fast-fashion formula for success combines frictionless, expeditious shopping in a highly-curated product environment offering scarce supply and new styles that rotate rapidly. Analysis by EDITED shows that Zara sells out new product drops in an average of 63 days, as compared with 119 for H&M.

The more quickly and efficiently a customer can navigate through the store to explore and find hidden gems, the better the experience. Zara nails that, while H&M requires the shopper to work to find what he or she wants.

H&M focuses on price; Zara on exchange for value

The old pricing formula, "Pile it high, sell it cheap!" worked well through the 20th century, but in the new experience economy, it has been replaced by the concept of exchange.

Exchanging dollars for product is no longer meeting the needs of today's shopper as they strive for deeper connections with the brand. Retailers must adapt to the changing consumer, where the top characteristic is VALUE=Time, Money, and Convenience.

Value is, of course, in the eye of the beholder. H&M's solution to its overstock problem is so old-school; chainwide fire sales to rid it of its excess inventory. But with cheap prices being one of its primary appeals for customers, how much lower can it afford to go to keep its "good fashion at a reasonable price" brand positioning intact?

Already H&M is scaping bottom, with nearly half of its womenswear tops priced in the $1-$20 bracket, according to EDITED's analysis, whereas Zara's favored womenswear tops price point is $20-$40.

Zara exhibits a deeper understanding of the entire value proposition it exchanges with the customers. Today, value is measured beyond price, but also in time and convenience. In Zara's case, the fast-fashion deliverable is available in the quantity, format, and time in which the customer needs the product. Zara expedites shopping online for those in "great need" of time thereby creating great value, all the while exposing shoppers to an environment that allows for high engagement. That translates into great value.

Brand value aligns customer's needs with a brand deliverable. For example, the top loyal customers for retailers typically account for 80 percent of sales. These brand loyalists are also less price-sensitive so strategies around tit-for-tat pricing, like H&M's, will never win.

Appealing to the loyal segment of the target market, like Zara does, allows for higher profit margins and caters to customers who seek out branded value.

Zara masters the art of branded value for their customers as they are not the cheapest in the fast-fashion arena, but they consistently deliver branded value of trend-right product at affordable prices. H&M still thinks in terms of product-price.

H&M pushes its promotions; Zara evangelizes

By making the brand experience meaningful and the exchange valuable, brands can tap the potential of its customers to evangelize the brand. It requires brands to create individual brand evangelists that will spread the word.

H&M is wedded to the idea of traditional paid advertising and push marketing strategies centered around capsule collections by outside designers. Today these strategies have become tired and formulaic. A recent collection by UK-based Erdem was a dud, despite being a designer brand favored by Kate Middleton, the Duchess of Cambridge.

Zara pulls its customers in and cultivates them as brand influencers.

Further, H&M recently found itself in a hornet's nest of bad publicity and social media outrage when it featured a young black boy modeling a sweatshirt emblazoned with "Coolest Monkey in the Jungle." In less than 24 hours it had over 18,000 retweets and 23,000 likes, or rather dislikes, as people were incensed by the insensitivity of the brand. Negative social media spreads like wildfire and can be the death of a brand.

Rather than push marketing out, Zara pulls its customers in and cultivates them as brand influencers to improve operations, services, and products. They become brand evangelists who share excitement about the brand with their networks. Shopper frequency at Zara is 2-to-3 times higher than traditional women's apparel, which indicates super loyalty to the brand. Active utilization of social media by the customer base further drives loyalty and a connection to the brand.

Zara has a highly evolved data infrastructure that allows for a super-efficient analysis of what's selling in the stores and what's being said on social media platforms. This data is used to improve various aspects of the business from product offerings to service enhancements. The two-way communication between the customer and Zara allows for continual improvement of products and services.

H&M thinks place; Zara is everyplace

Personal commerce is every place where the customers are, rather than only in the place the brand is physically present. This is the new distribution model for retailers today: Delivering the brand experience and products when and where the customer demands.

H&M has been slow to migrate sales online and sees a fix for the company in expanding its online presence. But that will fix only a small part of its problems. Its real estate strategies, at least in the U.S., have been uninspired and heavily weighted toward malls where over 80 percent of its stores are located. With nearly 600 U.S. stores, H&M faces off with all the other mall-based fashion retailers that are finding it increasingly difficult to gain traction in an already crowded market.

Zara, by contrast, is way ahead in its every place strategies. It has devoted significant time, money, and resources to synchronize online and offline commerce strategies. Linking a customer's shopping visit and providing access to inventory not present in that specific location allows shoppers to be in charge of their chosen destinations. It enables mobile connectivity as the conduit across various commerce channels and its mobile payment systems ease transactions on the customer's own terms. It is a big win for both the customer and the store staff.

And its precise location strategy is another aspect of its every place factor. It currently operates more than 2,000 Zara stores across 93 markets and 39 online markets. The flagship locations are located in the most critical markets that appeal to their most loyal shoppers. Zara dares to continually strengthen its portfolio of stores by closing unprofitable ones, opening new markets, and expanding sister brands in existing markets (Zara Home, Massimo Dutti).

Customer comes first

Under the old 4Ps school of marketing, everything focuses on the company and the brand – its Product, its Price, its Promotion, its Place. In the new 4Es approach to marketing, it is all about the customer – Experiences for the customer, Exchange with the customer, Evangelism through the customer, and being Every Place for the customer. In essence, the customer becomes the brand manager.

> *It's not about the brand (H&M), but about the customer (Zara)*

It's the unique advantage that Zara has over its competitors, chief of which is H&M. Zara actually listens and reacts to customer feedback to improve its products and services. That feedback is recognized as the brand's most valuable asset. In 2016, the service agents responded to more than 17 million customer inquiries. Zara's foundational principle of focusing on people with initiatives on diversity, respect, equal opportunity, work-life balance, and professional development further fosters a highly engaged workforce that translates into highly engaged interactions with customers. Additionally, over 60 percent of the Inditex workforce is 30 or younger aligning with the target market of the brand.

The result is the customer and the company work cooperatively together. In other words, Zara includes the customer in the decision-making process, whereas H&M dictates the decisions down to the customer, like in the old days when designers dictated fashion trends for the customer. But now the consumer calls the shots. Zara gets it, but H&M still has to learn it.

Pillars of New Luxury

In conclusion, it is important to understand just how vital HENRYs are to every brand's future in the high-end luxury market, as well as in every consumer-facing goods and services category.

On an individual basis, a HENRY household's spending power is dwarfed by that of the rich-now Ultra-affluent household. But as a group, the 30 million HENRYs combined contribute four-times more than Ultras to the consumer economy.

All told, Ultra-affluents, who make up 4 percent of total U.S. households, only account for some 10 percent of total consumer spending. HENRYs, by comparison, comprise roughly 40 percent of total consumer expenditures, leaving the middle-and-lower income households under

$100k annually making up the other 50 percent of consumer spending.

On average Ultra-affluents spend three-times more than households under $100k, and HENRYs spend twice as much. Yet due to their greater numbers, the HENRYs are the customers that every marketer needs and are even more important to luxury brands because the highest-spending customer in the future starts out as a HENRY.

Traditional Pillars of Luxury Must Evolve

The traditional pillars of luxury on which so many luxury brands are founded need to evolve as the young HENRYs continue to become the dominant force in the luxury market's future.

Here are the pillars of the new luxury market:

- **From exclusivity to elusiveness**

Exclusivity reeks of elitism and privilege, all qualities that repel rather than attract HENRYs. Instead of positioning new luxury brands around the old idea of exclusivity, luxury brands must evolve to being elusive and for that special individual that values that uniqueness.

Limited edition releases, special local offerings and special product releases or experiences grounded in a place and time are all on-trend for the HENRY perspective.

- **From a designers' creative expression to their own**

Designers may be the rock stars of traditional luxury, but in the world of new luxury, a designers' vision takes second place to the individuals' own.

Rather than taking a designers' endorsement that, "This is what I designed and you need," young HENRYs are the actual designers of their lives, their closets, and their homes. They are the curators of their own lifestyle and value new luxury brands that understand that the customers' personal vision is more important than the designer's name on the brand.

- **Think 'touch of the maker' instead of craftsmanship**

Traditional luxury brands make much of their craftsmanship. For HENRYs that craftsmanship must evolve into a more personal and intimate expression of craft.

Maker culture is taking hold among the next generation consumers, which is distinct from the designer culture of traditional luxury brands where the designer is many steps removed from the actual design going out the door and onto the shop floor.

HENRYs want to know not just that something is made to the highest standards of craftsmanship. They want to know who made it and how they made it. This story imparts deeper meaning to the brands the HENRYs are considering to make a part of their lives.

HENRYs want to feel the authentic touch of the maker and see their fingerprints on brand.

- **From product to experience**

Traditional luxury brands have historically led with product, with the experience of shopping and using the product secondary. In new luxury, that priority is reversed. HENRYs think first about the experience that the product will deliver along with the experience of searching out and finding it.

In the new luxury market, brands must turn their "product" into an experience. Apple made its name designing and selling innovative technology products, but senior vice president, Apple retail, Angela Ahrendts describes the Apple Stores as the company's "largest products," because they're now places where people come together to congregate and learn.

This technology giant understands how to turn its products into experiences for its customers.

- **Heritage and provenance give way to story**

Traditional luxury brands make the most of their heritage and provenance. Many of these brands are more than a century old and stay firmly rooted in their history.

HENRYs care less about how long a brand has been around or where it came from. Rather they are concerned with where the brand is today and where it is going tomorrow.

The founding story of a new luxury brand still is important, but less as a badge of honor and more as a reason why the brand is relevant to the customers' real-world concerns and needs today and tomorrow.

HENRYs look to the future and are not so interested in a brand's past. Rather they want to know how the brand fits into their future.

Move over sophistication and aesthetic; Get back-to-basics

Traditional luxury brands are elevated by an aesthetic of refined sophistication and elegance that only the chosen few can afford. New luxury goes in the other direction, putting priority on being real.

HENRYs are getting back-to-basics as their lifestyles get more harried and the culture more complicated. We see their preference for natural origins in the food they eat and the beauty products they use, but their desire for simplicity goes far beyond into all aspects of their lives.

Become a brand that HENRYs love

This book describes the new ways luxury brands must communicate and market to their future customers – The HENRYs. The need is to evolve the marketing model from the 4Ps – Product, Place, Price, Promotion - to the new

4Es where Experiences, Exchange, Everyplace and Evangelism are the new touchstones in customers' path to purchase.

Get More Insights

This book is excerpted from Pamela Danziger's *Meet the HENRYs: The Millennials that Matter Most for Luxury Brands* (Paramount Market Publishing, 2019). If you like what you've read and want to get more, *Meet the HENRYs* will give it to you.

In it, you'll get the story about the next-generation luxury consumers who have the means to buy luxury, thanks to their high income now with the potential for even higher earnings in the future. You'll understand their unique motivations that move young HENRYs into the market and to buy.

In addition, the book calls out unique opportunities where white space exists in the new luxury market ready to be filled, It also gives insight from profiles of new luxury brands that HENRYs love.

Julie Summers, in *Midwest Book Review*, said of Meet the HENRYs, "A groundbreaking and truly exceptional instruction manual offering a wealth of marketing insights and information, *Meet the HENRYs* is impressively well written, organized and presented, making it an ideal and highly recommended addition to community, corporate, and academic library business-management collections and supplemental studies reading lists. It should be noted for the personal reading lists of entrepreneurs, marketing managers, corporate executives, and non-specialist general readers with an interest in the subject."

And Neil Stern, senior partner at McMillanDoolittle, wrote, "For years we have been warning about the new wave of consumers who will change the way we shop. They are here now and they're called HENRYs. HENRYs have huge buying power but most importantly, a different set of values in how they think about and consume luxury. Pam's book is a treasure trove of insights and examples on how to appeal to these new consumers."

And Professor Niland Mortimer, at the Hult International Business School, said: "In the M.B.A. program we mostly teach from case studies and articles, but your book is the only really relevant and current source on luxury marketing to Millennials."

Get *Meet the HENRYs* and get ready for the luxury market of the future.

About the Author

Speaker, author, and market researcher Pamela N. Danziger is internationally recognized for her expertise on the world's most influential consumers: the American Affluent, including the HENRYs (high-earners-not-rich-yet) mass affluent.

As founder of Unity Marketing in 1992, Pam leads with research to provide brands with actionable insights into the minds of their most profitable customers. She is also a principal with Retail Rescue, which offers focused and effective consulting, training and mentorship in retail management, marketing, sales, and operations and partner in The American Marketing Group, which provides consultation and marketing support to home furnishings companies. In addition, she provides public relations consulting and content creation through Jill Schmidt PR.

Pam is a member of the renowned Leaders in Luxury + Design panel recognized by The Home Trust International. She received the Global Luxury Award for top luxury industry achievers presented at the Global Luxury Forum in 2007. She was named to *Luxury Daily*'s Luxury Women to Watch in 2013. She is a member of Jim Blasingame: The Small Business Advocate's Brain Trust and a contributing columnist to *The Robin Report* and Forbes.com.

Pamela N. Danziger

A prolific writer and blogger, Pam is author of ten books, including *Meet the HENRYs: Millennials that Matter Most to Luxury Brands*. Pam's bibliography includes a range of titles for Main Street retailers, as well as books for luxury marketers and luxury brands.

For retailers, there is *Shops that POP! 7 Steps to Extraordinary Retail Success*. For luxury marketers there is *Putting the Luxe Back in Luxury*. For interior designers and their to-the-trade partners, she offers *Marketing the Luxury of Interior Design*. And for home furnishings retailers and marketers there is *Home for HENRYs: Meet the New Customers Home Décor Marketers Are Searching For — High-Earners-Not-Rich-Yet*.

As a luxury market expert, Pam is frequently called on to share research-based insights with audiences and business leaders all over the world. She holds a B.A. in English Literature from Pennsylvania State University and an M.L.S. from University of Maryland.

Among her many television appearances and interviews, she has appeared on NBC's Today Show, CBS News Sunday Morning, CNN, Fox News, NPR's Marketplace, and CNN In the Money and was featured in the CNBC special "The Costco Craze: Inside the Warehouse Giant." She is frequently called upon by the Wall Street Journal, New York Times, USA Today, Associated Press and other business and consumer publications for commentary and analysis.

www.ingramcontent.com/pod-product-compliance
Lightning Source LLC
Chambersburg PA
CBHW070458220526
45466CB00004B/1871